Contemporary techniques of data mining using Meta-heuristic algorithms

Dr. Manju Bala

DEDICATION

To My Daughter Ira.

CONTENTS

ACKNOWLEDGMENTS

First and foremost. I would like to thank Almighty GOD for helping me and guiding me throughout my career and authoring this book.. And a special thanks to my mother Mrs. Dhanpati Devi, my father Mr. Prem Singh for allowing me to follow my ambitions throughout my childhood.

I also thank my wonderful children: Jiya, Ira, and Anjali, for always making me smile and for considerate on those weekend mornings when I was writing this book instead of spending time with them. I hope that one day they can read this book and understand why I spent so much time in front of my computer.

My family, including my husband and in-laws, has always supported me throughout my career and authoring this book and I really appreciate it.

1. INTRODUCTION

Data mining is the process of knowledge discovery. It associates research in many fields such as databases, statistics, artificial intelligence and machine learning [1]. Data mining can be carried out in two ways - Supervised learning and unsupervised learning. Supervised learning uses the known cases of well-defined patterns to get new patterns having feature of high interest and on the other hand in unsupervised learning no hypothesis is made on the relations among data sets to find out the pattern. The most important classification technique is clustering, in which a set of patterns are grouped into clusters based on some similarities [2].

Clustering is a popular analysis technique in data science, used in many applications and disciplines. Based on the values of various attributes of objects, it is used as an important tool and task to identify the homogeneous groups of the same.

Clustering can be of following two types – Hierarchal and Partitioning. Hierarchal clustering works on two techniques, division and agglomeration of data clusters. Division is breaking large clusters into smaller ones and agglomeration is merging small ones into nearest cluster. While in partition based clustering centre of each cluster is used to compute an objective function and the value of this function is optimized by updating the centre of clusters called as centroids. Clustering has a wide application in problems of data mining, data compression, pattern recognition and machine learning [3].

1.1. Basic Framework for Data Clustering

Traditional clustering algorithms consist of their own similarity metrics based on their nature. Some algorithms group the data set on the basis of density regions like DBSCAN and OPTICS, on the basis of distance like k-mean, on the basis of connectivity like hierarchical clustering. Over the period of time they all iterate to refine the solution towards Best cluster centroids. Now heuristic based algorithms are used for data clustering. They consist of search agents which represents candidate solution to the clustering problem. These candidate solutions are initialized by randomly 'k' cluster centroid in d-dimensional search space. Each heuristic algorithm moves the cluster centroid on the basis of their respective movement of candidate solution in order to achieve optimal results. This movement of cluster centroid carries on to fixed number of iteration to obtain optimal cluster centroid [4].

1.2. Swarm based optimization algorithms

The main motivation of the swarm based optimization algorithm is the natural phenomenon. Natural phenomenon is adopted for optimization purpose for meta-heuristic algorithms. Nature Inspired algorithms initially seeded with the random population in problem search space. These populations are evolved, combine and move over the fixed number of iterations to find the best solution. It is the main framework of the entire nature inspired optimization algorithm. These algorithms only differ by the movement or the evolution of its population for obtaining optimizes results. For example there are algorithms like GA [5] (genetic algorithm) in which the concept of survival of the fittest is adopted by GA to find the best solution. Population are operated by two operators: mutation and crossover to evolve or move the population. PSO [6] (Particle swarm optimization) was inspired by individual thinking and social behavior of particles (bird) to move the swarm in search space. Every particle on the basis of its neighbor interaction and its local best position move to obtain global best position of swarm. The entire nature based algorithms consist of two main concepts:

✓ **Exploration**: Exploration is the process of finding the promising areas for the optimization problem. These areas consist of potential solutions.

✓ **Exploitation**: Exploitation is used to convergence of the solution to the promising area find in the Exploration phase.

Proper balance has to maintain between exploration and exploitation phase so that solution does not trap in local optima and solution will be obtain in optimize time. So a proper transition is used to move the candidate solution toward global optima. Nowadays meta-heuristic algorithms are widely in many optimization problems. Many researches are going on to proposing nature inspired optimization problems and modifying previous heuristic algorithm in order to make them efficient.

K-means is the widely used partitioning based clustering algorithm. It uses a square-error objective function based on the sum of distances between the data points. Its biggest drawback is that it tends to converge to local optimum solution around the initial search positions. To solve the problem of local optima, many nature inspired and population based algorithms such as – Swarm

Intelligence Algorithms, Artificial Neural Networks, Genetic algorithms and Evolutionary Algorithms are being used. Based on combining K-mean and evolutionary algorithms many hybrid optimization algorithms also have been proposed.

2 . REVIEW OF EXISTING CLUSTERING ALGORITHMS

With the evolution of soft computing and the meta heuristic algorithms there was a huge performance gain in the field of optimization. Clustering problem is nothing but a problem of getting cluster center by optimizing the function based on some similarity measure. So I. De Falco, A. Della Cioppa and E. Tarantino, et al [7], in their paper, for Applied Soft Computing, "Facing classification problems with Particle Swarm Optimization" , described how to solve the classification problem using a swam based algorithm and performed the clustering on the instances of multiclass datasets. It states that the results of clustering are better than the other algorithms with the same performance magnitude and it suitably challenge the two-class problems. But it doesn't conclude on the performance of clustering data having more than two classes.

Nature inspired metaheuristic algorithm solved the main problem of local optima stagnation in classical clustering algorithms by generating multiple set of search agents in the search space. This gives a large search option which avoids the local optima and evaluates each initial set of agents using the fitness function (objective function). These algorithms have methods to remove the most unfit set of agent, which leads to gradual convergence towards global optima.

Abdolreza Hatamlou, et al. [8], in his work describes a nature inspired algorithm based on Black Hole Phenomenon. It is used to solve the problem of clustering. He used the Iris, Wine, CMC, cancer and Vowel datasets to show that black hole algorithm outperforms the other algorithm. Two main benefits of this algorithm are that it doesn't require any parameter tuning and due to simple structure it is easy to implement.The result of this algorithm is that it yields to better results when compared to other clustering algorithms such as K-means, PSO & GSA.

DervisKaraboga, CelalOzturk, et al [9] in 2009, in his paper "A novel clustering approach: Artificial Bee Colony (ABC) algorithm". This paper introduced an optimization algorithm based on the intelligent behaviour of foraging in honey bees. Using the thirteen UCI machine learning datasets this paper demonstrates the application of this algorithm for clustering. It compared the results of clustering to the PSO and other nice benchmark algorithm on the basis of classification error percentage of the multivariate datasets.

Due to large number of search agent initialization these metaheuristic algorithms tends to slow down when used to optimize a function operating on a dataset with large number of instances and attributes. This problem is addressed by combining the features of two or more algorithms to create a hybrid algorithm.

TaherehHassanzadeh and Mohammad Reza Meybodi, et al [10], proposed a hybrid clustering approach which uses Firefly algorithm and K-means algorithm. In this work centroid are evaluated using the nature of fireflies and then refining these results using the K-means. K-means helps in speeding up the execution and Firefly algorithm helps in avoiding the local optima. To do so they seeded the initial value of K-mean centroids using the values obtained by firefly algorithm.GA Clustering

Genetic Algorithm

Genetic algorithm is inspired by biological phenomena in living beings. In GA data sets encoded as string and this string collection produces the population within search space. Random population in initial stage is seeded in search space and for each string and objective function or fitness function is associated. On probabilistic basis we find the some strings which go over mutation and crossover [12] which generates new population. These two operators are adopted from biological theory. This process continues over a period of time (iterations) to get the Optimization results.

Clustering Using GA:-

The optimization ability of GA is adopted in clustering the 'n' number of data set into 'k' number of fixed clusters. The Euclidean distance has been taken as similarity metric for assigning object to cluster. The objective function or fitness of each string or chromosome is modelled as cluster distance that should be minimized. Each string represents by the sequence of real number and the length of every string is 'NxK' words where 'K' is number of clusters centroid and 'n' is N-dimensional space. Every string (chromosome) is randomly initialized by 'k' random points. Mathematically the metric for clustering is given as:

$$M\ (C1,\ C2,...,Ck) = \sum_{t=1}^{k} ||xj - zi||$$

Now fitness computation is two stage processes. At

first stage for every chromosome and for each data point we find the nearest cluster centroid on the basis of Euclidean distance. Finally assigned that data point to nearest cluster centroid as

$$\|xi\text{-}zj\| < \|xi\text{-}zp\|, p = 1,2,\ldots k, \text{ and } p!=j.$$

After all the data points are assigned in second Stage calculation of mean point of all the cluster centers encoded in the chromosome are replaced with calculated mean which is calculated according to the following equation:

$$Z^* = (1/ni) \sum xj, i=1,2,\ldots,k.$$

Now selection of some chromosome will be done on the basis of their fitness value and roulette wheel mechanism adopted for the chromosomes which goes under the mating pool. In mating pool two operation are applied on the chromosome, they are mutation and crossover. In crossover to parent chromosome exchange their information to generate two child. In mutation each chromosome undergoes with some modification that results in new chromosome. These operation are responsible for generation of new and strong population. Finally when condition criteria is met up we stop this genetic biological process.

Pseudo Code for GA

Begin

1. t=0
2. initialize population p(t)
3. compute fitness p(t)
4. t = t+1
5. if termination criterion achieved go to step 10
6. select p(t) from p(t-1)
7. crossover p(t)
8. mutate p(t)
9. goto step 3
10. output best and stop.

Black Hole based Clustering

This algorithm is based on the phenomenon of collapsing of a star into a dark void. In 1967 John Wheeler coined the term Black Hole. The high gravitational pull causes the shrinking of mass and even light rays can't escape this pull. The boundary to which this gravitational pull affects the passing nearby objects is called as Schwarzschild radius and it is denoted by following equation:

$$R = \frac{2GM}{c^2} \tag{1}$$

Where G is Gravitational Constant, M is mass and C is speed of light.

This algorithm introduces the black hole method used in [13] into the PSO. It generated random particles near best solution and then it updates the particle position either using PSO or new mechanism based on the two random generated numbers. At first it generates the random population of candidate solutions in the search space as black holes and stars. These stars are absorbed by the black holes causing the movement. The changes in the position of stars are reflected using following equation:

$$X_i(t + 1) = X_i(t) + rnad \times (X_{BH} - X_i(t)) \quad i = 1, \quad (2)$$

Where Xi(t)and XBH(t) is the position of star and black hole respectively at iteration t. rand is the random number generated in the interval of [0,1]. N represents the number of stars or candidate solution.

There are events when a star crosses the event horizon of the black hole which leads to death of that star by getting pulled into the void. With the death of one star another star is generated randomly to start new search and to keep candidate solutions constant.

In Black Hole Algorithm the radius of event horizon is calculated by following equation:

$$R = \frac{f_{BH}}{\sum_{i=1}^{N} f_i} \quad (3)$$

Where f_{BH} is black hole's fitness value and f_i the star's fitness. N is the number of stars.

Psuedo Code:

Initialize the star population

Loop

> i. Evaluate the objective function for each star.
> ii. Select the star with best fitness value as black hole.
> iii. Update the Location of stars using equation (2)
> iv. Swap the position of star with black hole if it has lower fitness value.
> v. Create new star randomly if one crosses the event horizon.
> vi. If termination criteria met exit the loop.

End Loop

Classification with Particle Swarm Optimization

This algorithm by I. De Falco, A. Della Cioppa and E. Tarantino uses PSO [13-15] for clustering of multivariate datasets. For a dataset of C classes and N attributes clustering problem is a problem if finding the position of C centroids [8].

In generated population i^{th} individual can be represented as follows:

$$\vec{p}_i^1,.....\vec{p}_i^C,\vec{v}_i^1,......,\vec{v}_i^C \qquad (4)$$

Where $\vec{p}_i^j$ is the position vector having N real number and $\vec{v}_i^j$ is the N real number velocity vector. Each individual in population have $2 \times C \times N$ components.

It has three objective functions. The first objective function φ_1 consists of two steps;

1. Each individual training set is assigned to nearest class centroid C.

2. It calculates the fitness by evaluating the percentage of incorrectly assigned dataset i.e. if class $CL(\vec{x}_j)$ assigned to $\vec{x}_j$ and class $CL_{Known}(\vec{x}_j)$ known of $\vec{x}_j$ is different.

$$\varphi_1(i) = \frac{100.0}{D_{Train}} \sum_{j=1}^{D_{Train}} \delta(\vec{x}_j) \qquad (5)$$

Where D_{Train} represent the number of instances in the training dataset.

$$\delta(\vec{x}_j) = \begin{cases} 1 & if \ CL(\vec{x}_j) \neq CL_{Known}(\vec{x}_j) \\ 0 & otherwise \end{cases} \qquad (6)$$

$\varphi_1$will vary in the interval [0.0, 100.0].

Second objective function is the sum of all the Euclidian distance of training dataset, denoted as φ_2.

$$\varphi_2(i) = \frac{1}{D_{Train}} \sum_{j=1}^{D_{Train}} d(\vec{x}_j, \vec{p}_i^{CL_{known(\vec{x}_j)}}) \tag{7}$$

Third objective function φ_3 also have two, first step is same as of φ_1. Second step combines the above two objective function linearly.

$$\varphi_3(i) = \frac{1}{2}\left(\frac{\varphi_1(i)}{100.0} + \varphi_2(i)\right) \tag{8}$$

Algorithm is executed using these three objective functions and denoted as different versions: $PSO - \varphi_1$, $PSO - \varphi_2$ and $PSO - \varphi_3$.

Results obtained shows that $PSO - \varphi_3$gave the best result among all three versions. Out of 13 sample datasets in 10 datasets, it gave least classification error percentage.

Hybrid Firefly and K-means Algorithm

Fireflies flashes light in short rhythmic pattern. This helps them to communicate with each other and it also attracts other insects to prey on them. Based on this behaviour of fireflies, YANG in 2008 introduces an algorithm by the name of Firefly Algorithm [17]. One firefly moves toward another firefly which is brighter. Attractiveness is directly proportional to brightness and inversely proportional to the distance. Attractiveness is given by following equation [10]:

$$\beta(r) = \beta_0 e^{-\gamma r^2} \tag{9}$$

Where, γ is source's light absorption coefficient and β_0 is attractiveness at $r = 0$.

Distance between two fireflies is evaluated using Cartesian formulae and represented as $r_{i,j}$.

$$r_{i,j} = \|x_i - x_j\| = \sqrt{\sum_{k=1}^{d} (x_{i,k} - x_{j,k})^2} \tag{10}$$

Movement of fireflies is defined by following equation:

$$X_i = x_i + \beta_0 e^{-\gamma r_{ij}^2}(x_j - x_i) + \alpha\left(rand - \frac{1}{2}\right) \tag{11}$$

In original version of Firefly Algorithm due to influence of brighter firefly on weaker it tends to avoid global best in some cases. To overcome this drawback a modified version of Firefly Algorithm is formulate with the help of K-means algorithm. In the modified algorithm one firefly in affected by nearest brighter firefly as well as by firefly corresponding to global best.

New modified movement equation is:

$$X_i = x_i + (\beta_0 e^{-\gamma r_{ij}^2} (x_j - x_i)$$
$$+\beta_0 e^{-\gamma r_{ij}^2 g_{best}} (x_j - x_i) + \alpha(rand - \frac{1}{2})$$

(12)

Author uses the results obtained by firefly algorithm to seed the initial population in K-means Algorithm. In traditional K-means algorithm initial population is generated randomly. This causes K-means to get stuck in the local optima. But when seeded by the results of Firefly gives K-means initial population a tightly bound value initialization. K-mean minimises its objective function i.e. decreases the sum of Euclidian distance of clusters and its instances. K-means uses following equation to get sum of Euclidean distances:

$$Dis(X_p, Z) = \sqrt{\sum_{i=1}^{d} (X_{pi} - Z_{ji})}$$
(13)

To refine the cluster centre it uses following equation:

$$Z_j = \frac{1}{n_j}\left(\sum_{\forall X_p \in j} X_p\right)$$
(14)

Where, n_j is the number of instances in the cluster j and Z_j is the centre of the cluster

Pseudo Code:

Initialize fireflies with random K*D centres
  While (t<max generation)
    For i=1: n (all n fireflies)
    For j=1: n (all n fireflies)

Calculate objective function of each firefly by equation 13,

If (ij>ii)

Move firefly I toward j based on equation 12 to refine positionof fireflies (clusters centre)

End if

End for j

End for i

Ranks the fireflies and find the current best to update current best to next iteration

End while

Rank the fireflies and find global best and extract the position of global best

Repeat

Initialize the k-means centre with position of global best

Allocate each vector to a cluster by equation 13,

Refined the clusters by equation 14

Do until predefined iteration.

Artificial Bee Colony Algorithm for Clustering

In 2005, D. Karaboga proposed a stochastic algorithm based in the swarming nature of honey bees [18]. It simulates a colony of honey bees in which there are three kinds of bees:

- Employed Bees- Going to the food source which was visited earlier.
- Onlooker Bees- Decides which food source to accept and reject.
- Scouts Bees- Goes is different directions to find new sources.

Food Sources are the possible solution of problem and nectar content of the food represents the fitness of the source and it can be calculated using:

$$fit_i = \frac{1}{1 + f_i} \qquad (15)$$

Where, f_i is:

$$f_i = \frac{1}{D_{Train}} \sum_{j=1}^{D_{Train}} d(x_j, p_i^{CL_{Known}(x_j)}) \tag{16}$$

Onlooker Bees select a food source in the on the basis of the probability value of it and it can calculated as:

$$p_i = \frac{fit_i}{\sum_{n=1}^{SN} fit_n} \tag{17}$$

Where, SN is the total number of food sources and it is equal to total number of employed bees.

To generate position of a possible candidate food from an old source, ABC uses following equation:

$$v_{ij} = z_{ij} + \emptyset_{ij}(z_{ij} - z_{kj}) \tag{18}$$

Where $\emptyset_{ij} \in [-1,1]$, $k \in \{1,2,......,SN\}$ and $j \in \{1,2,....,D\}$ generated randomly and both k and i must be different.

Scout bees replace an old abandoned food

source and replaces with z_i, this can be defined as:

$$z_i^j = z_{min}^j + rand(0,1)(z_{max}^j - z_{min}^j) \qquad (19)$$

Pseudo Code:

Load training Sample

Generate the initial population z_i

Evaluate the fitness (f_i) of the population

Set cycle to 1

Repeat

    For each employed bee {

    Produce new solution v_i by using (18)

    Calculate the value f_i

Apply greedy selection process}

Calculate the probability value p_i, for the solution (z_i) by (5)

For each onlooker bee {

    Select a solution z_i depending on p_i

    Produce new solution v_i

    Apply greedy selection process}

If there is an abandoned solution for the scout the replace it with a new solution which will be randomly produced by (19)

Memorize the best solution so far

Cycle = cycle+1

Until cycle=MCN

3.OPTIMIZED CLUSTERING ALGORITHM BASED ON K-MEANS AND ANTILION APPROACH

K-Means Clustering Algorithm

In 1967, MacQueen proposed an unsupervised learning algorithm, by the name of K-Means Algorithm [19], which addressed the problem of clustering. This algorithm provides a fast and easy to implement way to divide the data instances into predefined k number of clusters. Its main aim is to get centroids for all k clusters. As the end results rely heavily on the initialization of the centroids so it is advised to choose these very carefully. In the early grouping stage all the centroids are set to remote position in the search space and after initialization of centroids, all instances of dataset must be assigned to the nearest centroid. After the first step of groupage, we will recalculate the centroid. Second step will start with re-assigning the points to the newly adjusted centroids. These steps will continue to be repeated until there is no change in centroids i.e. there is any movement in the position of the centroids. This algorithm minimizes the objective fiction, Square error function:

$$J = \sum_{j=1}^{k} \sum_{i=1}^{n} \left\| x_i^{(j)} - C_j \right\|^2 \tag{20}$$

Where $\left\| x_i^{(j)} - C_j \right\|^2$ is the distance between $x_i^{(j)}$ and C_j. n is the total number of instances in the dataset.

K-Means is good simple and fast clustering algorithm. It has been used in numerous works to extend its capabilities e.g. $fuzzy\ feature\ vector$. It have been proved that this algorithm will always terminate but it may not yield best result always. Due to its high fluctuating nature which depends upon the initial centroid position, it is advised to run multiple instances of K-means to get a global optimal result.

Algorithm Steps:

1. Place K points into the space represented by the objects that are being clustered. These points represent initial group centroids.

2. Assign each object to the group that has the closest centroid.

3. When all objects have been assigned, recalculate the positions of the K centroids.

Repeat Steps 2 and 3 until the centroids no longer move. This produces a separation of the objects into groups from which the metric to be minimized can be calculated.

Algorithm Analysis:

K-Means is clustering algorithm which work on the greedy principle. It partitions the n data samples in to k clusters to minimize the sum of Euclidian distance of all data samples from their cluster centres. MajorDrawbacks of this algorithm are:

- No proper method to initialize. Generally done randomly.

- Due to high dependency on the initial centres it may get stuck to suboptimal values, only quick solution is to execute it multiple times.

- Accuracy changes with change in number of cluster (k).

- In many cases it tends to get stuck to local or sub optima.

Antilion Optimization Algorithm

In recent years, trends have shown a huge development in the area of soft computing with the rise of nature inspired meta heuristic algorithms [21-23]. Due to the use of stochastic operators in the process it doesn't get suffer from local optima stagnation which was the major issue of deterministic algorithms [24-27]. Local optima stagnation is the case when algorithm gets entrapped in the local optimal values causes the loss of global optimal values. As the large data sets have large number of local optimal solutions which leads to failure of deterministic algorithms. Stochastic family of optimization algorithms include the algorithm having stochastic operators including evolutionary algorithms.

Evolutionary algorithms [28] work interactively on randomly generated population in the search space, this population is known as candidate solution. It improves the candidate solutions on each iteration until a termination criteria is fulfilled. These improvements are based on exploration of search space and exploitation of results obtained. Exploration guarantees that algorithm will not stuck in local optima and continue to search for more global optimal values while on the exploitation ensures the convergence towards the suitable optimal value [29].

One of the main reasons behind the popularity of evolutionary algorithms is that the process of optimization is independent of problem. There are large numbers of problems that are yet to be solved and we know there is no silver bullet for that [30]. A single algorithm can't solve each and every problem efficiently and accurately. So, many algorithms have been proposed to solve these problems. Most popular algorithms are: Genetic Algorithm (GA) [31][32], Particle Swarm Optimizer (PSO) [32], Ant Colony Optimization (ACO) [34] and Evolutionary Programming (EP)[35].

Ant Lion optimization algorithm is inspired by the hunting nature of the insect belonging to the Myrmeleontidate family. Antlion prey on the ants and hunt them by digging a cone shaped pit in the ground. At the bottom of the pit it sits and waits of an ant to fall into it. It throws the sand outside the cone so that ant gets pushed into the bottom and can't escape the trap. Size of trap varies according to the hunger of the antlion. These hunting steps are mimicked in this algorithm [36-40].

(a)   *(b)*

Figure 1 (a) Antlion (b) Hunting Pit

First it generates a random population of n ants and antlions into the search space having d dimensions and saved as M_{Ant} and $M_{Antlion}$ matrix:

$$M_{Ant} = \begin{bmatrix} A_{1,1} & A_{1,2} & \cdots & \cdots & A_{1,d} \\ A_{2,1} & A_{2,2} & \cdots & \cdots & A_{2,d} \\ \vdots & \vdots & \vdots & \vdots & \vdots \\ \vdots & \vdots & \vdots & \vdots & \vdots \\ A_{n,1} & A_{n,2} & \cdots & \cdots & A_{n,d} \end{bmatrix}$$

$$M_{Antlion} = \begin{bmatrix} AL_{1,1} & AL_{1,2} & \cdots & \cdots & AL_{1,d} \\ AL_{2,1} & AL_{2,2} & \cdots & \cdots & AL_{2,d} \\ \vdots & \vdots & \vdots & \vdots & \vdots \\ \vdots & \vdots & \vdots & \vdots & \vdots \\ AL_{n,1} & AL_{n,2} & \cdots & \cdots & AL_{n,d} \end{bmatrix}$$

Then it will calculate the initial fitness of each ant and antlion using some objective function (f). These values are saved into an array of size d as:

$$M_{OA} = \begin{bmatrix} f([A_{1,1}, A_{1,2}, ..., A_{1.d}]) \\ f([A_{2,1}, A_{2,2}, ..., A_{2.d}]) \\ \vdots \\ f([A_{n,1}, A_{n,2}, ..., A_{n.d}]) \end{bmatrix}$$

$$M_{OAL} = \begin{bmatrix} f([AL_{1,1}, AL_{1,2}, ..., AL_{1.d}]) \\ f([AL_{2,1}, AL_{2,2}, ..., AL_{2.d}]) \\ \vdots \\ f([AL_{n,1}, AL_{n,2}, ..., AL_{n.d}]) \end{bmatrix}$$

Random movement of ants is simulated using following stochastic function:

$$X(t) = [0, cumsum(2r(t_1 - 1)), cumsum(2r(t_2 - 1)),$$
$$...cumsum(2r(t_n - 1))]$$

Where, $r(t) = \begin{cases} 1 \; if \; rand > 0.5 \\ 0 \; if \; rand \leq 0.5 \end{cases}$ (21)

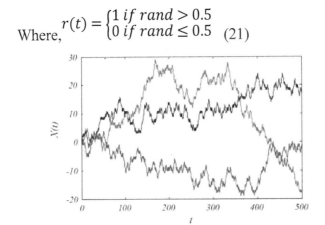

Figure 2 Three Random Walks

To limit the movement of ant into the boundary of search space it needed to be normalized:

$$X_i^t = \frac{(X_i^t - a_i) \times (d_i^t - c_i^t)}{(b_i - a_i)} + c_i^t \qquad (22)$$

Where, a_i is the minimum & b_i is the maximum of ith variable and c_i is the minimum & d_i is the maximum of ith variable in t^{th} iteration.

To implement sliding of ant towards antlion we limit the random movement of ants by decreasing the upper and lower bound in each iteration using:

$$c^t = \frac{c^t}{I} \qquad (23)$$

$$d^t = \frac{d^t}{I} \qquad (24)$$

Where, $I = 10^w \frac{t}{T}$ and $w = 2$ when $> 0.1T$, $w = 3$ when $t > 0.5T$, $w = 4$ when $t > 0.75T$, $w = 5$ when $t > 0.9T$, $w = 6$ when $t > 0.95T$. T is number of iterations.

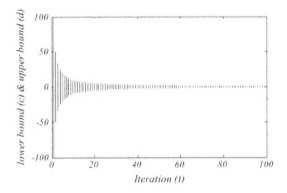

Figure 3 Adaptive Upper and Lower bound

Finally we simulate the catching of ant by antlions. If an ant becomes fitter than antlion it will be consumed and antlion will build new trap at the location of ant.

$$Antlion_j^t = Ant_i^t \; if \; f\left(Ant_i^t\right) > f(Antlion_j^t)$$
$$(25)$$

To reflect the elitism in the ant movement it must be affected by best antlions (global) as well as antlion selected by roulette wheel (local). We take average these movements.

$$Ant_i^t = \frac{R_A^t + R_E^t}{2} \qquad (26)$$

35

Results shown in the figure depicts that for multimodal functions it have high convergence rate and it covers the search space to a great extent.

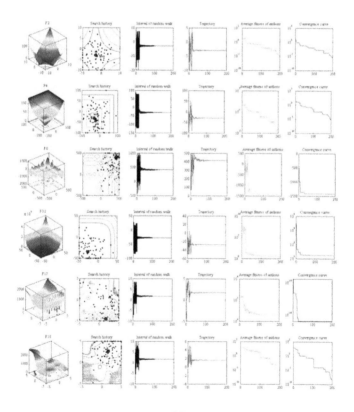

Figure 4 Search Space Exploration and

Convegence

Analysis of Antlion Optimizer:

This algorithm showed a high rate of convergence on simple as well as composite test functions. These functions test both the exploration and exploitation capabilities of the algorithm. ALO showed a balanced exploration and exploitation capabilities. This makes ALO a potentially capable solution to problems with complex calculation and high dimensionality. When observing convergence curve it can be seen that with the increase of iteration accuracy of global optimum accelerates. The main disadvantage of this algorithm is that it cost a high amount of time for a search space having large number of dimensions. Such as for a dataset with 200 dimensions we need approximately 5000 iterations to achieve desired global optima.

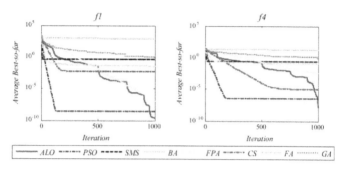

Figure 5 Convergence Comparison of ALO to

others

Pseudo Code:

Initialize the first population of ants and antlions randomly

Calculate the fitness of ants and antlions

Find the best antlions and assume it as the elite (determined optimum)

While the end criterion is not satisfied

    For every ant

        Select an antlion using Roulette wheel

        Update c and d using equations Eq. (23) and (24)

        Create a random walk and normalize it using Eq. (21) and (22)

        Update the position of ant using (26)

    End for

Calculate the fitness of all ants

Replace an antlion with its corresponding ant it if becomes fitter (Eq. 25)

Update elite if an antlion becomes fitter than the elite

End while

Return elite

Optimized Algorithm:

, we have seen that there are some basic problems with original clustering algorithms that they either suffer from local optima entrapment or there is performance degradation. Another problem that persist there is that initialization in evolutionary algorithms have very high degree of randomization because of a set of search agents getting scattered into search space, which is again have large number of dimensions.

To counter these problematic drawbacks of these traditional clustering and optimization algorithms I have proposed a hybrid algorithm based on K-Mean Clustering and Antlion Optimization Algorithm. This hybrid algorithm is used to solve the clustering problem and named as

Hybrid Antlion Clustering Algorithm. It addressed the local optima problem of K-Mean as well as provides performance gain to original Antlion Optimization Algorithm. But key advantage of this problem is that besides removing these drawbacks it can also perform clustering successfully on datasets which have overlapping instances.

Proposed algorithm is based on the antlion optimization algorithm, explained in the previous chapter. In the original algorithm where antlions and ants are initialized in the search space using the random initialization function into the boundaries. But in the proposed algorithm to antlions are seeded using the results of K-Means algorithm.

There are n number of agents (antlions) are needed to be initialized in the form of vector consisted of k number of cluster centres of d number of dimensions each.

$$\{z_1^1, z_2^1, ..., z_d^1, z_1^2, z_2^2, ..., z_d^2, ..., z_1^k, z_2^k, ..., z_d^k\}$$

So each antlions position consists of $d \times k$ number of dimensions. i.e. $N = d \times k$, where N is the dimensionality of each antlion and there will be n number of antlions. While initializing it will require n iteration of K-means algorithm to be executed. This will bound the search space cluster centres by antlions into a pre-optimized field of search.

Objective function:

To perform the clustering on the dataset using this algorithm the following objective function is used as the fitness function:

$$f(w,z) = \sum_{i=1}^{N} \sum_{j=1}^{k} w_{ij} \|x_i - z_j\|^2$$

This function uses the Euclidean distance as the similarity matrix for the clustering. According to this matrix, a point closer to a cluster centre belongs to that cluster.

Algorithm Parameters:

- Number of antlions: 40
- Numbers of ants: 40
- Number of iterations: 500
- Upper bound and Lower bound of each attribute is the upper bound and lower bound of the corresponding attribute in dataset

Data Set used in Clustering:

Widely used dataset in clustering problem are usually multivariate. These are available in therepository of the machine learning databases [41]. These dataset have more than two dimensions. Some of widely used data sets are:

- ***IRIS Dataset:***

Iris dataset [42] consist of a flower which having three types of breed. It is perhaps the best known database to be found in the pattern recognition literature. The data set contains 3 classes of 50 instances each, where each class refers to a type of iris plant. Each dataset has four attributes. One class is linearly separable from the other 2; the latter are NOT linearly separable from each other.

Predicted attribute: class of iris plant.

.Attribute Information:

1. Sepal length in cm.
2. Sepal width in cm.
3. Petal length in cm.
4. Petal width in cm
5. Class:
   - Iris Setosa
   - Iris Versicolour
   - Iris Virginica
   - *Wine dataset:*

These data are the results of a chemical analysis of wines grown in the same region in Italy but derived from three different cultivars. The analysis determined the quantities of 13 constituents found in each of the three types of wines. The initial data set had around 30 variables, but for some reason I only have the 13 dimensional version. It consist a list of what the 30 or so variables were, but a.) I lost it, and b.), I would not know which 13 variables are included in the set. It consist of 178 instances and 3 types of wine. Each classes have 59, 71, 48 instances of each class.

Attribute Information:

The attributes are

1. Alcohol
2. Malic acid
3. Ash
4. Alcalinity of ash
5. Magnesium
6. Total phenols
7. Flavanoids
8. Nonflavanoid phenols
9. Proanthocyanins
10. Color intensity
11. Hue
12. OD280/OD315 of diluted wines
13. Proline

In a classification context, this is a well posed problem with "well behaved" class structures. A good data set for first testing of a new classifier, but not very challenging.

• *Glass Dataset:*

The study of classification of types of glass was motivated by criminological investigation. At the scene of the crime, the glass left can be used as evidence...if it is correctly identified. This glass dataset consist of 9 attributes and 6 types of glasses which results in 6 cluster.the number of instaces consist in all cluster is 70,76,13,9 and 29.

Attribute Information:

1. RI: refractive index
2. Na: Sodium (unit measurement: weight percent in corresponding oxide, as are attributes 4-10)
3. Mg: Magnesium
4. Al: Aluminum
5. Si: Silicon
6. K: Potassium
7. Ca: Calcium

8. Ba: Barium

9. Fe: Iron

10. Type of glass: (Clusters)

- Building windows float processed
- Building windows non float processed
- Vehicle windows float processed
- Containers
- Tableware
- Headlamps

- ***Cancer Dataset:***

This is one of three domains provided by the Oncology Institute that has repeatedly appeared in the machine learning literature. This Breast cancer data set includes 444 instances of one class and 239 instances of another class. The instances are described by 9 attributes, some of which are linear and some are nominal.

Attribute Information:

1. Class: no-recurrence-events, recurrence-events

2. Age

3. Menopause

4. Tumor-size

5. Inv-nodes

6. Node-caps

7. Deg-malig

8. Breast:

9. Breast-quad:

10. Irradiat:.

- ***CMC Dataset:***

This dataset is a subset of the 1987 National Indonesia Contraceptive Prevalence Survey. The samples are married women who were either not pregnant or do not know if they were at the time of interview. The problem is to predict the current contraceptive method choice (no use, long-term methods, or short-term methods) of a woman based on her demographic and socio-economic characteristics.

Attribute Information:

1. Wife's age (numerical)
2. Wife's education (categorical) 1=low, 2, 3, 4=high
3. Husband's education (categorical) 1=low, 2, 3, 4=high
4. Number of children ever born (numerical)
5. Wife's religion (binary) 0=Non-Islam, 1=Islam
6. Wife's now working? (Binary) 0=Yes, 1=No
7. Husband's occupation (categorical) 1, 2, 3, 4
8. Standard-of-living index (categorical) 1=low, 2, 3, 4=high
9. Media exposure (binary) 0=Good, 1=Not good

10. Contraceptive method used (class attribute) 1=No-use, 2=Long-term, 3=Short-term

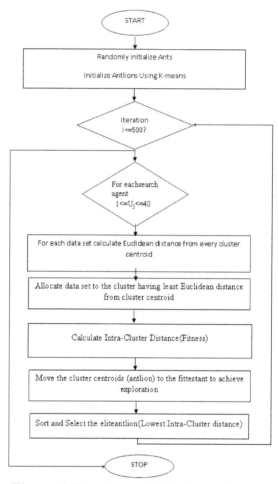

Figure 6 Flowchart ALO Clustering

4 MULTI-VERSE OPTIMIZER ALGORITHM

The big bang theory [25] discusses that our universe starts with a massive explosion. According to this theory, the big bang is the origin of everything in this world, and there was nothing before that. Multi-verse theory is another recent and well-known theory between physicists. It is believed in this theory that there are more than one big bang and each big bang causes the birth of a universe. The term multi-verse stands opposite of universe, which refers to the existence of other universes in addition to the universe that we all are living in. Multiple universes interact and might even collide with each other in the multi-verse theory. The multi-verse theory also suggests that there might be different physical laws in each of the universes. We chose three main concepts of the multi-verse theory as the inspiration for the MVO algorithm: white holes, black holes, and wormholes. A white hole has never seen in our universe, but physicists think that the big bang can be considered as a white hole and may be the main component for the birth of a universe. It is also argued in the cyclic model of multi-verse theory [26] that big bangs white holes are created where the collisions between parallel universes occur. Black holes, which have been observed frequently, behave completely in contrast to white wholes. They attract everything including light beams with their extremely high gravitational force [27]. Wormholes are those holes that connect different parts of a universe together. The wormholes in the multi-verse theory act as time/space travel tunnels where objects are able to travel instantly between any corners of a universe (or even from one universe to another). Conceptual models of these three key components of the multi-verse theory are illustrated in Fig. 7.

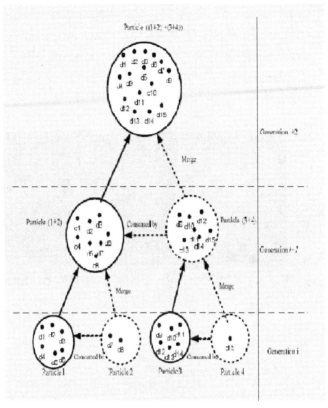

Figure 7 Evolutionary Particle Swarm Optimization clustering

Every universe has an inflation rate (eternal inflation) that causes its expansion through space [28]. Inflation speed of a universe is very important in terms of forming stars, planets, asteroids, black holes, white holes, wormholes, physical laws, and suitability for life. It is argued in one of the cyclic multi-verse models [29] that multiple universes interact via white, black, and wormholes to reach a stable situation. This is the exact inspiration the MVO algorithm, which is conceptually and mathematically modelled in the following subsection.

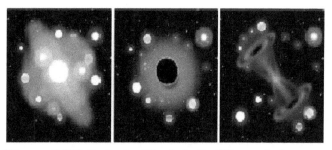

Figure 8 White hole, Black hole, Worm hole

MVO algorithm

As discussed in the preceding section, a population-based algorithm divides the search process into two phases: exploration versus exploitation. We utilize the concepts of white hole and black hole in order to explore search spaces by MVO. In contrast, the wormholes assist MVO in exploiting the search spaces. We assume that each solution is analogous to a universe and each variable in the solution is an object in that universe. In addition, we assign each solution an inflation rate, which is proportional to the corresponding fitness function value of the solution. We also use the term time instead of the iteration in this paper since it is a common term in multi-verse theory and cosmology.

During optimization, the following rules are applied to the universes of MVO:

1. The higher inflation rate, the higher probability of having white hole.
2. The higher inflation rate, the lower probability of having black holes.
3. Universes with higher inflation rate tend to send objects through white holes.
4. Universes with lower inflation rate tend to receive more objects through black holes.
5. The objects in all universes may face random movement towards the best universe via wormholes regardless of the inflation rate. The conceptual model of the proposed algorithm is illustrated in Fig. 8. This figure shows that the objects are allowed to move between different universes through white/black hole tunnels. When a white/black tunnel is established between two universes, the universe with higher inflation rate is considered to have white hole, whereas the universe with less inflation rate is assumed to own black holes.

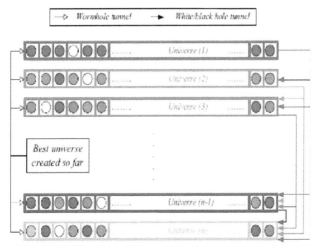

Figure 9 Conceptual model of the proposed MVO algorithm (I(U1) I(U2).....I(Un-1)[I(Un))

The objects are then transferred from the white holes of the source universe to black holes of the destination universe. This mechanism allows the universes to easily exchange objects. In order to improve the whole inflation rate of the universes, we assume that the universes with high inflation rates are highly probable to have white holes. In contrary, the universes with low inflation rates have a high probability of having black holes. Therefore, there is always high possibility to move objects from a universe with high inflation rate to a universe with low inflation rate. This can guarantee the improvement of the average inflation rates of the whole universes over the iterations. In order to mathematically model the white/black hole tunnels and exchange the objects of universes, we utilized a roulette wheel mechanism. At every iteration, we sort the universes based of their inflation rates and chose one of them by the roulette wheel to have a white hole. The following steps are done in order to do this.

Assume that

$$
U = \begin{bmatrix}
x_1^1 & x_1^2 & \cdots & x_1^d \\
x_2^1 & x_2^2 & \cdots & x_2^d \\
\vdots & \vdots & \vdots & \vdots \\
x_n^1 & x_n^2 & \cdots & x_n^d
\end{bmatrix}
$$

where d is the number of parameters (variables) and n is the number of universes (candidate solutions):

$$
x^j_i = \begin{cases} x^j_k & r1 < NI(U_i) \\ \\ x^j_i & r1 >= NI(U_i) \end{cases} \qquad \text{eq 8}
$$

where x^j_i indicates the jth parameter of ith universe, U_i shows the ith universe, $NI(U_i)$ is normalized inflation rate of the ith universe, r1 is a random number in [0, 1], and x^j_k indicates the jth parameter of kth universe selected by a roulette wheel selection mechanism.

The **PseudoCode** for this part are as follows:
SU=Sorted universes
NI=Normalize inflation rate (fitness) of the universes
for each universe indexed by i
    Black_hole_index=i;
        for each object indexed by j
                r1=random([0,1]);
                if $r1 < NI(Ui)$
White_hole_index=RouletteWheelSelection(-NI);
U(Black_hole_index,j)= SU(White_hole_index,j);
                end if
        end for
end for

the selection and determination of white holes are done by the roulette wheel, which is based on the normalized inflation rate. The less inflation rate, the higher probability of sending objects though white/black hole tunnels. Please note that -NI should be changed to NI for the maximization problems. The exploration can be guaranteed using this mechanism since the universes are required to exchange objects and face abrupt changes in order to explore the search space. With the above mechanism, the universes keep exchanging objects without perturbations. In order to maintain the diversity of universes and perform exploitation, MVO consider that each universe has wormholes to transport its objects through space randomly. In Fig. 8, white points represent transferred objects through the wormholes. It may be observed that the wormholes randomly change the objects of the universes without consideration of their inflation rates. In order to provide local changes for each universe and have high probability of improving the inflation rate using wormholes, assuming wormhole tunnels are always established between a universe and the best universe formed so far. The formulation of this mechanism is as follows:

$$X^j i = \begin{cases} \begin{cases} Xj+TDR*((ubj-lbj)*r4+lbj) & r2<WEP \\ Xj-TDR*((ubj-lbj)*r4+lbj) & eq(9) \\ X^j i & r2>=WEP \end{cases} \end{cases}$$

where Xj indicates the jth parameter of best universe formed so far, TDR is a coefficient, WEP is another coefficient, lbj shows the lower bound of jth variable, ubj is the upper bound of jth variable, $x^j i$ indicates the jth parameter of ith universe, and r2, r3, r4 are random numbers in [0, 1].

The **pseudocode** are as follows (assuming that ub and lb indicate upper bound and lower bound of the variables):

for each universe indexed by i

    for each object indexed by j

        r2=random([0,1]);

        if r2<Wormhole_existance_probability

        r3= random([0,1]);
        r4= random([0,1]);

        if r3<0.5
U(i,j)=Best_universe(j) + Travelling_distance_rate
    * ((ub(j) -lb(j)) *r4 + lb(j));
Else
U(i,j)= Best_universe(j) - Travelling_distance_rate
    * ((ub(j) -lb(j)) *r4 + lb(j));

        end if

      end if

    end for

end for

It may be inferred from the pseudo codes and mathematical formulation that there are two main coefficients herein: wormhole existence probability (WEP) and travelling distance rate (TDR). The former coefficient is for defining the probability of wormhole's existence in universes. It is required to increase linearly over the iterations in order to emphasize exploitation as the progress of optimization process. Travelling distance rate is also a factor to define the distance rate (variation) that an object can be teleported by a wormhole around the best universe obtained so far. In contrast to WEP, TDR is increased over the iterations to have more precise exploitation/local search around the best obtained universe. Wormhole existence and travelling distance rates are illustrated in Fig. 3. The adaptive formula for both coefficients are as follows:

$$WEP = min + l* ((max - min) / L)$$

$$TDR = 1-(pow(1, 1/p))/(pow(L, 1/p))$$

where min is the minimum value, max is the maximum value, 1 indicates the current iteration, and L shows the maximum iterations, p defines the exploitation accuracy over the iterations. The higher p, the sooner and more accurate exploitation/local search. Note that WEP and TDR can be considered as constants as well, but we recommend adaptive values according to the MVO methodology. In the MVO algorithm, the optimization process starts with creating a set of random universes. At each iteration, objects in the universes with high inflation rates tend to move to the universes with low inflation rates via white/ black holes. Meanwhile, every single universe faces random teleportations in its objects through wormholes towards the best universe. This process is iterated until the satisfaction of an end criterion (a pre-defined maximum number of iterations, for instance).

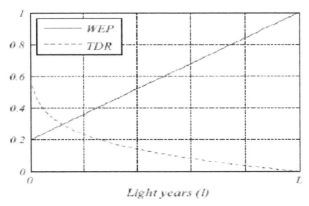

Light years (l)

Figure 4 Worm hole existence probability versus Travelling distance rate

The computational complexity of the proposed algorithms depends on number of iterations, number of universes, roulette wheel mechanism, and universe sorting mechanism. Sorting universe is done in every iteration, and we employ the Quicksort algorithm, which has the complexity of O (n log n) and O(n^2) in the best and worst case, respectively. The roulette wheel selection is run for every variable in every universe over the iterations and is of O (n) or O(log n) based on the implementation. Therefore, the

overall computational complexity is as follows:

O(MVO)=O(l(O(quicksort)+n*d*(O(roulette wheel)))) eq(12)

$$O(MVO)=O(l(n^2 + n*d*\log(n))) \qquad eq(13)$$

where n is the number of universes, l is the maximum number of iterations, and d is the number of objects.

To see how the proposed algorithm theoretically has the potential to solve optimization problems, some observations are as follows:

- White holes are more possible to be created in the universes with high inflation rates, so they can send objects to other universes and assist them to improve their inflation rates.

- Black holes are more likely to be appeared in the universes with low inflation rates so they have higher probability to receive objects from other universes.

This again increases the chance of improving inflation rates for the universes with low inflation rates.

- White/black hole tunnels tend to transport objects from universes with high inflation rates to those with low inflation rates, so the overall/average inflation rate of all universes is improved over the course of iterations.

- Wormholes tend to appear randomly in any universe regardless of inflation rate, so the diversity of universes can be maintained over the course of iterations.
- While/black hole tunnels require universes to abruptly change, so this can guarantee exploration of the search space.
- Abrupt changes also assist resolving local optima stagnations.
- Wormholes randomly re-span some of the variables of universes around the best solution obtained so far over the course of iterations, so this can guarantee exploitation around the most promising region of the search space.
- Adaptive WEP values smoothly increase the existence probability of wormholes in universes. Therefore, exploitation is emphasized during optimization process.
- Adaptive TDR values decrease the travelling distance of variables around the best universe, a mechanism for increasing the accuracy of local search over the iterations.

- The convergence of the proposed algorithm is guaranteed by emphasizing exploitation/local search proportional to the number of iterations.

Pseudocode of MVO Clustering:

1. Initialize each Universe to contain Nc randomly selected cluster centroids.

2. For t = 1 to tmax do

   a) For each Universe Ui do

   b) For each data vector $\mathbf{z}p$

   I. calculate the Euclidean distance $d(\mathbf{z}p, \mathbf{m}ij)$ to all cluster centroids Cij

   II. assign $\mathbf{z}p$ to cluster Cij such that $d(\mathbf{z}p, \mathbf{m}ij) = \min_{c=1;\_\_;Nc} \{d(\mathbf{z}p; \mathbf{m}ic)\}$

   III. calculate the fitness using equation (13)

      (c) Move the cluster centroid on the basis for equation 13

      (d) Find the Best Universe and move the cluster's centroid on the basis of equation 13

      3. Stop.

5 RESULTS: ANTILION OPTIMIZATION ALGORITHM

Five benchmark datasets from UCI depository with a variety of complexity are used to evaluate the performance of the proposed approach. Thedatasets are Iris, Wine, Glass, Wisconsin Breast Cancer and Contraceptive Method Choice (CMC), which are available in the repository of the machine learning databases [41]. BelowTable 1summaries the main characteristics of the used datasets.

The performance of the ALO-clustering algorithm is compared against well-known and the most recent algorithms reported in the literature, including K-means , particle swarm optimization, and gravitational search algorithm . The performance of the algorithms is evaluated and compared using the Sum of intra-cluster distances as an internal quality measure: The distance between each data object and the center of the Corresponding cluster is computed and summed up.

Clearly, the smaller the sum of intra-cluster distances, the higher the quality of the clustering. The sum of intra-cluster distances is also the evaluation fitness in this work.

As seen from the results the ALO Clustering algorithm achieved the best results among all the algorithms. For the *Iris dataset*, the best, worst, and average solutions obtained by ALO Clustering are *96.6555* for all iterations, which are better than the other algorithms.

For the *Wine dataset*, the ALO algorithm achieved the optimum value of *16292.9233*, whichis significantly better than the other test algorithms.

As seen from the results for the *Glass dataset*, the ALO clustering algorithm is far superior to the other algorithms. The worst solution obtained by the ALO clusteringalgorithm on the Glass dataset is *203.7370*, which is much better than the best solutions found by the other algorithms.

For the ***Cancer dataset***, the ALO clustering algorithm outperformed the K-means, PSO and GSA algorithms with an optimal value of ***2964.3870***.

For the ***CMC dataset***, the proposed ALO clustering algorithm reached an average of ***5532.2785***, while other algorithms were unable to reach this solution even once within 50 runs.

From the above results, we can say that in five of the test datasets the proposed ALO clustering algorithm is superior to the other test algorithms. It can find high quality solutions. In other words, the ALO clustering algorithm converges to global optimum in all the runs while the other algorithms may get trapped in local optimum solutions. Only in the Cancer dataset did one of the algorithms (GSA) reach a better solution than the ALO clustering. Even in this dataset, the ALO clustering algorithmreached high quality clusters compared to the other three test algorithms.

Table 1 Main characteristics of the test datasets

Dataset	Number of clusters	Number of features	Number of data objects
Iris	3	4	150
Wine	3	13	178
Glass	6	9	214
Cancer	2	9	683
CMC	3	9	1473

Table 2 The sum of intra-cluster distances obtained by algorithms on different datasets.

Dataset	Criteria	K-Means	PSO	GSA	ALO
Iris	Best	97.32592	96.87935	96.68794	96.65555
	Average	105.72902	98.14236	96.731051	96.65555
	Worst	128.40420	99.76952	96.824632	96.65555
Wine	Best	16,555.67	16,304.48	16,313.87	16292.9233
	Average	16,963.044	16,316.27	16,374.30	16293.2847
	Worst	23,755.049	16,342.78	16,428.86	16295.2048
Glass	Best	215.67753	223.90546	224.98410	203.7370
	Average	227.97785	230.49328	233.54329	205.9341
	Worst	260.83849	246.08915	248.36721	210.1411
Cancer	Best	2986.96134	2974.48092	2964.76394	2964.3870
	Average	3032.24781	2981.78653	2964.66312	2964.3873
	Worst	5216.08949	3053.49132	2993.24458	2964.3876
CMC	Best	5542.18214	5539.17452	5542.27631	5532.2785
	Average	5543.42344	5547.89320	5581.94502	5532.5929
	Worst	5545.33338	5561.65492	5658.76293	5532.7791

Graph based comparison of K-mean and ALO Clustering is discussed in this section. ALO clustering completely outperform the K-mean clustering algorithm. The graph consists of number of iteration vs optimization in each iteration. This comparison has been done on five benchmark functions like Iris, Wine and Glass. The graph shown below:

1. **Iris dataset:** Graph shown below is the Intra-cluster distance vs number of iteration is given in which ALO clustering has optimal value of 96.6555 and k-mean clustering provides 97.3259over the 500 number of iterations when applied on iris dataset.

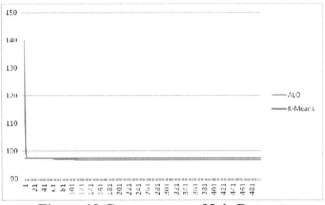

Figure 10 Convergence of Iris Dataset

2. **Glass dataset**: Graph shown below is the Intra-cluster distance vs number of iteration is given in which ALO clustering has optimal value of 203.7370 and k-mean clustering provides 215.8526 over the 500 number of iterations when applied on glass dataset.

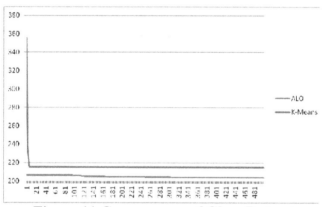

Figure 11 Convergence of Glass Dataset

3. **Wine Dataset**: Graph shown above is the Intra-cluster distance vs number of iteration is given in which ALO clustering has optimal value of 16292.9233 and k-mean clustering provides

16,555.67 over the 500 number of iterations when applied on wine data.

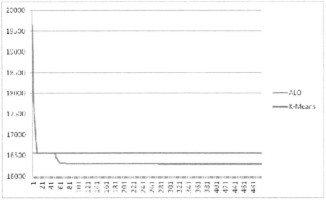

Figure 12 Convergence of Wine Dataset

6 RESULTS: MVO Algorithm

The performance of the MVO-clustering algorithm is compared against well-known and the most recent algorithms reported in the literature, including K-means , particle swarm optimization, and gravitational search algorithm . The performance of the algorithms is evaluated and compared using the Sum of intra-cluster distances as an internal quality measure: The distance between each data object and the center of the Corresponding cluster is computed and summed up. Clearly, the smaller the sum of intra-cluster distances, the higher the quality of the clustering. The sum of intra-cluster distances is also the evaluation fitness in this work.

As seen from the results the MVO Clustering algorithm achieved the best results among all the algorithms. For the Iris dataset, the best, worst, and average solutions obtained by MVO Clustering are 96.65589, 96.65681, and 96.6605, respectively, which are better than the other algorithms. For the Wine dataset, the MVO algorithm achieved the optimum value of 16293.41995, which is significantly better than the other test algorithms. As seen from the results for the Glass dataset, the MVO clustering algorithm is far superior to the other algorithms. The worst solution obtained by the MVO clustering algorithm on the Glass dataset is 213.95689, which is much better than the best solutions found by the other algorithms. For the Cancer dataset, the MVO clustering algorithm outperformed the K-means, PSO and GSA algorithms. For the CMC dataset, the proposed MVO clustering algorithm reached an average of 5533.63122, while other algorithms were unable to reach this solution even once within 50 runs. From the above results, we can say that in five of the test datasets the proposed MVO clustering algorithm is superior to the other test algorithms. It can find high quality solutions. In other words, the MVO clustering algorithm converges to global optimum in all the runs while the other algorithms may get trapped in local optimum solutions. Only in the Cancer dataset did one of the algorithms (GSA) reach a better solution than the MVO clustering. Even in this dataset, the MVO clustering algorithm reached high quality clusters compared to the other three test algorithms.

The sum of intra-cluster distances obtained by algorithms on different datasets.

1. **Iris dataset:** Graph shown below is the Inta-cluster distance vs number of iteration is given in which MVO clustering has optimal value of 96.6005 and k-mean clustering provides 97.3259 over the 100 number of iterations when applied on iris dataset.

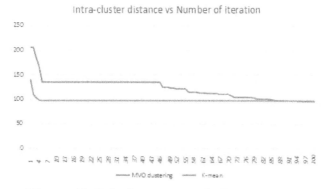

Figure 13 Iris dataset graph: Intra-cluster distance vs Number of iteration

2. **Glass dataset**: Graph shown below is the Intra-cluster distance vs number of iteration is given in which MVO clustering has

optimal value of 203.861 and k-mean clustering provides 215.8526 over the 100 number of iterations when applied on glass dataset.

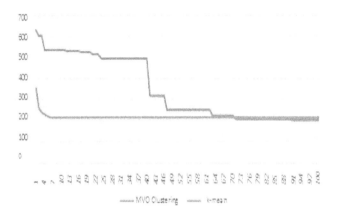

Figure 14 Glass dataset graph: Intra-cluster distance vs Number of iteration

3. **Wine Dataset:** Graph shown above is the Inta-cluster distance vs number of iteration is given in which MVO clustering has optimal value of 16299.01 and k-mean clustering provides 16,555.67 over the 100 number of iterations when applied on wine data.

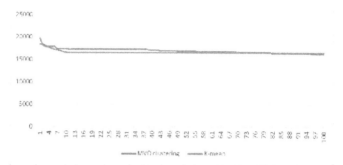

Intra-cluster distance vs Number of iteration

Figure 15 Wine dataset graph: Intra-cluster distance vs Number of iteration

7 CONCLUSION

Data clustering is a most popular and effective data mining technique and is attracting more researchers as the amount of data and need for information management increases. Clustering techniques aim to group similar data into identical clusters in an optimal manner. To achieve optimality in the process and in the results various optimization techniques have been used to improve one or another aspect of clustering. One of such optimization based technique is Antlion Optimization Algorithm. Our aim in this work is to tackle these problems by proposing a novel generation based algorithm called ALO-clustering algorithm.

The algorithm was tested on benchmark data and results are compared with the benchmark k-means clustering algorithm as well as PSO-clustering algorithms, Gravitational search clustering. The experimental ALO-clustering results are better than k-means clustering, PSO-clustering and GSA clustering. The idea presented in this work possess new research directions by utilizing the hunting nature of antlions to hunt down ants and update the position of its trap according to the fitness of previous hunting leads to findingan optimal cluster centroid of the cluster problem.

Some of the issues which need to be addressed in order to enhance the performance and generalization of the algorithm are as follows.

- Selection of the number of agents
- Initialization of the Universe
- Attribute evolution during exchange of objects.
- The criteria for maturity (strength) of the Universe.

- Selection of the number of agents and number of suitable iterations
- Initialization of the Antlions
- Movement around the antlion
- The criteria for similarity in clusters other than Euclidean Distance.

References

[1] A. Jain, R. Dubes, Algorithms for Clustering Data, Prentice-Hall, Englewood Cliffs, NJ, 1998.

2] M. Sarkar, B. Yegnanafayana, D. Khemani, A clustering algorithm using an evolutionary programming-based approach, Pattern Recogn.Lett. 18 (1997) 975–986.

[3] J. Han, M. Kamber, Data Mining: Concepts and Techniques, Academic Press, 2001

[4] W. Barbakh, Y. Wu, C. Fyfe, Review of clustering algorithms, in: Non-Standard Parameter Adaptation for Exploratory Data Analysis, Springer, Berlin/ Heidelberg, 2009, pp. 7–28.

[5] John H (1992) Holland, adaptation in natural and artificial systems. MIT Press, Cambridge

[6] Kennedy J, Eberhart R (1995) Particle swarm optimization. In:Proceedings of IEEE international conference on neural networks, pp 1942–1948

[7] I. De Falco a, A. Della Cioppa b, E. Tarantino a, Facing classification problems with Particle Swarm Optimization Applied Soft Computing 7 (2007) 652–658

[8] AbdolrezaHatamlouî, Black hole: A new heuristic optimization approach for data clustering, Information Sciences 222 (2013) 175–184

[9] DervisKaraboga, CelalOzturk, A novel clustering approach: Artificial Bee Colony (ABC) algorithm, Applied Soft Computing 11 (2011) 652–657

[10] TaherehHassanzadeh Mohammad Reza Meybodi, A New Hybrid Approach for Data Clustering using Firefly Algorithm and K-means, The 16th CSI International Symposium on Artificial Intelligence and Signal Processing (AISP 2012)

[12] L. Davis (Ed.), Handbook of Genetic Algorithms, Van Nostrand Reinhold, New York, 1991.

[13] J. Zhang, K. Liu, Y. Tan, X. He, Random black hole particle swarm optimization and its application, in: 2008 IEEE International Conference Neural Networks and Signal Processing, ICNNSP, 2008, pp. 359–365.

[14] R.C. Eberhart, J. Kennedy, A new optimizer using particle swarm theory, in: Proceedings of the Sixth International Symposium on Micro Machine and Human Science, IEEE Press, Piscataway, NJ, 1995, pp. 39–43.

[15] J. Kennedy, R.C. Eberhart, Particle Swarm Optimization, in: Proceedings of the IEEE International Conference on Neural Networks IV, vol. 4, IEEE Press, Piscataway, NJ, 1995, pp. 1942–1948.

[16] R.C. Eberhart, Y. Shi, Computational Intelligence: Concepts to Implementations, Morgan Kaufmann, 2003.

[17] X. L. Yang, Q. Song and W. B. Zhang, "Kernel-based Deterministic Annealing Algorithm For Data Clustering", in IEEE Proceedings on Vision, Image and Signal Processing, Vol. 153, pp. 557-568, March 2007.

[18] D. Karaboga, An idea based on honey bee swarm for numerical optimization, Technical Report-TR06, Erciyes

University, Engineering Faculty, Computer Engineering Department, 2005.

[19] MacQueen JB (1967) Some methods for classification and analysis of multivariate observations. In: 5th Berkeley symposium on mathematical statistics and probability, vol 1. University of California Press, Berkeley, pp 281–297

[20] Forgy EW (1965) Cluster analysis of multivariate data: efficiency versus interpretability of classifications. In: Biometric society meeting, Riverside

[21] Blum C, Puchinger J, Raidl GR, Roli A. Hybrid metaheuristics in combinatorial optimization: a survey. Appl Soft Comput 2011;11:4135–51.

[22] Boussaïd I, Lepagnot J, Siarry P. A survey on optimization metaheuristics. Inform Sci 2013;237:82–117.

[23] Gogna A, Tayal A. Metaheuristics: review and application. J ExpTheorArtifIntell 2013;25:503–26.

[24] Bianchi L, Dorigo M, Gambardella LM, Gutjahr WJ. A survey on metaheuristics for stochastic combinatorial optimization. Nat Comput: Int J 2009;8:239–87.

[25] Cornuéjols G. Valid inequalities for mixed integer linear programs. Math Program 2008;112:3–44.

[26] Avriel M. Nonlinear programming: analysis and methods. Courier Dover Publications; 2003.

[27] Land AH, Doig AG. An automatic method for solving discrete programmin problems. In: 50 Years of integer programming 1958–2008. Springer; 2010. p. 105–32.

[28] Back T. Evolutionary algorithms in theory and practice. Oxford Univ. Press; 1996.

[29] Talbi E-G. Metaheuristics: from design to implementation, vol. 74. John Wiley & Sons; 2009.Holland JH.Genetic algorithms.Sci Am 1992;267:66–72.

[30]Wolpert DH, Macready WG. No free lunch theorems for optimization. IEEE Trans EvolComput 1997;1:67–82.

[31] Holland JH, Reitman JS. Cognitive systems based on adaptive algorithms. ACM SIGART Bull 1977. p. 49–49.

[32] Eberhart RC, Kennedy J. A new optimizer using particle swarm theory. In: Proceedings of the sixth international symposium on micro machine and human science; 1995. p. 39–43.

[33] Colorni A, Dorigo M, Maniezzo V. Distributed optimization by ant colonies. In: Proceedings of the first European conference on artificial life; 1991. p. 134–42.

[34] Fogel LJ, Owens AJ, Walsh MJ. Artificial intelligence through simulated evolution; 1966.

[35] Yao X, Liu Y, Lin G. Evolutionary programming made faster. IEEE Trans EvolComput 1999;3:82–102.

[36] Scharf I, Subach A, Ovadia O. Foraging behaviour and habitat selection in pitbuilding antlion larvae in constant light or dark conditions. AnimBehav 2008;76:2049–57.

[37] Griffiths D. Pit construction by ant-lion larvae: a cost-benefit analysis. J AnimEcol 1986:39–57.

[38] Scharf I, Ovadia O. Factors influencing site abandonment and site selection in a sit-and-wait predator: a

review of pit-building antlion larvae. J Insect Behav 2006;19:197–218.

[39] Grzimek B, Schlager N, Olendorf D, McDade MC. Grzimek's animal life encyclopedia. Michigan: Gale Farmington Hills; 2004.

[40] Goodenough J, McGuire B, Jakob E. Perspectives on animal behavior. John Wiley & Sons; 2009.

[41] C.J. Merz, C.L. Blake, UCI Repository of Machine Learning Databases. <http://www.ics.uci.edu/-mlearn/MLRepository.html>.

[42] R.A. Fisher, The use of multiple measurements in taxonomic problems, Ann. Eugenics 3 (1936) 179}188.